Printed in the United States of America
Published By: Legacy Voice Productions (Loganville, GA)

© Copyright 2023 by Ann Marie Barnes

All rights reserved. This book or parts thereof may not be reproduced in any form, stored in a retrieval system, or transmitted in any form by any means-electronic, mechanical, photocopy, recording, or otherwise-without prior written permission of the author, except as provided by United States of America copyright law.

Written by: Ann Marie Barnes

I would like to share "Blessed Kids" children's book with you and your families. Blessed Kids was published, dedicated, and designed on behalf of my grandson, Jahsir A'Mare Johnson born 2/8/2023, when I found out I was going to be a GiGi (grandmother).

My first thought was to create a book that would give positive affirmations to my grandson daily. I believe that our children require a great seed(s) to be sown from the beginning of life. Those seeds consist of Faith, Love, and Positive Affirmations.

Cover & Illustrations by: Fatima Zeeshan

ISBN: 978-1-960179-03-6

Welcome to the World Jahsir

I dedicate this book to you.

Seeds of Life,
Seeds of Grace,
Seeds of Joy,
And
Seeds of Love!

Sincerely GG Ann Marie

I will be great.

Journal: My Happy Days

_____

_____

_____

_____

_____

THANK YOU

www.ingramcontent.com/pod-product-compliance
Lightning Source LLC
Chambersburg PA
CBHW062024050526
44107CB00105B/868